JON CORBETT

MEMBER MACHINE

The Ultimate Guide to Membership Sites, Learn All the Insider Secrets and Best Tips on How to Build a Successful Membership Site

Descrierea CIP a Bibliotecii Naţionale a României
JON CORBETT
    MEMBER MACHINE. The Ultimate Guide to Membership
Sites, Learn All the Insider Secrets and Best Tips on How to
Build a Successful Membership Site / Jon Corbett – Bucharest:
Editura My Ebook, 2021
    ISBN

JON CORBETT

MEMBER MACHINE

**The Ultimate Guide to Membership Sites, Learn
All the Insider Secrets and Best Tips on How to
Build a Successful Membership Site**

My Ebook Publishing House
Bucharest, 2021

TABLE OF CONTENTS

INTRODUCTION

What do palm reading, pet grooming, senior travel and sports cars all have in common? They are all subjects that have membership websites dedicated to them. What does that mean? It means that every single month a clever Internet entrepreneur is spending a little bit of time adding content and information to their website about such issues as those mentioned above, and then receiving a steady stream of income from the people who subscribe to the informative site in order to get all kinds of special and relevant materials as well as deals on products at discounted rates.

Sounds like an easy way to make a living, right? Well, it can be, but ONLY if the site and all of the marketing are done properly. The focus of this e-book will be on identifying and implementing the types of strategies and procedures necessary to obtaining true success with a membership website.

The thing to remember is that all modern Internet entrepreneurs have instant access to the information and the many hard lessons learned by others who have worked over the past decade or more to succeed with an online business. Many of the Internet's most successful business people have their own websites, eBooks and "webinars" that cover the most valuable subjects and some are entirely free to enjoy.

Modern entrepreneurs and business people also have a huge number of tools that make it simple to pull together a workable and appealing website through which the memberships and associated products can be sold.

This book is going to address all of the secrets needed to create one, or even dozens, of the most successful exclusive membership communities in the online world. Additionally, if the steps are followed, the Internet professional will find that their sites will virtually run themselves and become self-sustaining businesses.

Chapter 1 – It's an Online Business

Some Basic Facts about Online Business Success

Although you may be contemplating whether or not you will open a membership website, you should always remember that it is going to be an online business just as much as any other big or major online retailer or service. Because of this you will have to make sure you register the business legally according to your local laws, and you will also have to lay the groundwork necessary for an online business too.

This usually means you will have to own the right equipment (computer, scanner, fax, etc.), have a website or an account with a web hosting company, and you are going to have to dedicate some time to learning how an online business works. For example, you will determine quite quickly that you need an ecommerce website with the appropriate banking or merchant payment arrangements. You will also discover that you are going to have to understand how to update and change the appearance of your website on a frequent basis as well.

There are many other technical issues that we will address as we proceed through this work, but it is important to begin the entire process of building your membership website on the clear understanding that it is going to take some basic steps that have very little to do with the products you will be working to sell. This is a frequent stumbling block because many people are eager to spread the word about their product or information.

Before progressing any farther along, it is also a good idea to ask yourself if you are going to work alone or if you might benefit from taking on a partner? The power of the Internet makes it easy to work with people on different continents and within different industries. You may want to think about the amount of time it is going to take for you to handle administrative tasks, website updates and marketing. If you feel that this may be impossible, it is a good idea to scout out some support or even a partnership – many Internet success stories begin with good partnerships.

With all of this in mind, we can now begin looking at what it takes to succeed with a membership website.

The Learning Curve

When we use the phrase the "learning curve" we are going to mean that you will have to accept that you will make some missteps and mistakes in the process of building and refining your membership website. Just take them for what they are...learning experiences! Even negative feedback or wrong choices can be used to improve your business.

For instance, you are going to have to understand that the marketing trends that were super- successful in, say, 2005 may not be so great in 2009. New trends appear every day, and it will be entirely up to you to keep up with this information.

Always remembering that you are a "worldwide" entrepreneur is also going to make it easier to accept that browsing patterns and buying patterns as well as specific interest in certain information is going to be fluid. You will soon understand that only fluid websites can succeed in such an environment as well.

For example, take the idea of "direct mail". This was once the king of the marketing world, and it relied on pre-paid mailing lists that might arrive in an office on pre-printed labels or on a formatted computer disk. They cost a bit of money, and were often pitched as being targeted to the right consumers for the industry or product. Although this was something popular in the late 1990s, today it is looked at as a marketing dinosaur.

Instead, there are online ad sites and direct "email" lists among many other Internet tools for marketing and sales. Following trends is an important and valuable way to identify the best methods for contacting your markets. More importantly, however, is implementing a self- assessment program on marketing campaigns and advertisements. There are a huge variety of software packages and Internet tools that can help a dedicated professional to measure their success, and this is something that should be done every day of the week in order to reduce losses on failing ads or to improve the look or content of a website.

A Brief Look at the Tools

So, what are these tools? Well, for the membership website professional, the key tool is their actual website. This is something that will include several "landing pages", a sales letter, products pages, and information available only to registered and paying members. In order to have such a powerful tool, however, the website owner is going to have to address some key issues.

The first is their personal level of skill in creating a good-looking and workable website. There are hundreds of web hosting companies offering complete templates and easy to use tools, and if this is something in the budget it is a highly recommended choice.

Remember, however that the site is also going to have the "members only" areas, which must be designed to prevent access by non-members and by those whose memberships have been cancelled or which have lapsed. To better address these issues, we will dedicate part of the "Getting Started" chapter to the development of the website.

The other tools that are essential to success will be those used for marketing and advertising. These will include well-written emails, powerful "adwords", and a plan for paid advertising and traffic acquisition. These too are issues to be covered in a few succeeding chapters, and if you would like to skip ahead, please see the "Basic Formula" and "Getting Started" sections.

Finally, the basic tools must also include the five key ways of bringing on new memberships and expanding profit potentials for the site, and these are regular audio workshops or "webinars", developing resources, member discounts, reprint and resale rights, and selling wholesale memberships. All five topics are going to be thoroughly reviewed in the succeeding sections of this work.

The Focus

Consider that membership websites offer everything from mentoring and one on one coaching; access to authoritative articles, libraries and information on specific issues and industries; results of formal or interesting studies and results; and even serve as a virtual meeting place for like-minded individuals.

What are some examples? Well, almost everyone knows about the organization called "Consumer Reports", and that is a membership site with members-only access to the detailed reports and studies. It is successful because it offers a well-developed and "niche" product.

This means they give something to their customers that is not readily or easily found anywhere else, and that is the key to success with any membership site.

It all begins when you select your product or subject. This is something of enormous significance for two key reasons: first, if the subject is too obscure or of little interest to a broader community, you may not see any sales where memberships and eBooks or programs are concerned. Second, if the subject is of little interest to you, the entrepreneur, you will not have the right level of enthusiasm or ongoing knowledge about it.

For these reasons it is important to pick subjects and products that will have a wide and popular appeal. Remember, however, that you can expand your subject to cover a broader public. For instance, if you want to develop a membership-only Internet community about palm reading, you may want to also include "psychics", "supernatural powers" and other associated concepts in your advertising and in your web content. This is just a simple example of how a subject can be enhanced to have much wider all around appeal.

The point is that all membership sites have a single, strong fact in common – people are willing to pay to access them. This means specialized and valid information, merchandise or materials unavailable elsewhere.

Now, we'll begin to dig into the details of developing your membership website, and it begins with the essential tools, techniques and attitudes discussed in the next chapter.

Chapter 2 – The Basic Formula

If you look at the way every successful Internet entrepreneur works, you will see that they put a lot of time and attention into building a successful website, and then they seem to just step back a bit and let the site "do its thing". This is only possible because a certain basic formula has been followed, and though it may at first seem very simplistic, it is in fact quite involved and requires serious thought.

It all begins with the relevant market and the right advertising.

Testing the Markets

So, you have that idea or subject and you want to build a membership website around it. That's great, but first you would be wise to invest a realistic amount of time and money in testing your general markets.

Pay Per Click

This is best done through something like GoogleAdWords, or another Pay Per Click (PPC) advertising site. (NOTE: Many of the popular social networking sites also sell PPC ads, and this is a very affordable approach to developing some marketing information and plans.)

You will have to choose the right "keywords" and compose the brief text for the ad, and this takes a bit of research in advance. What are keywords? They are the terms most frequently entered into a search engine when a consumer is looking for information, merchandise or a specific website. They are usually embedded in a website's text through special tags (known as Meta tags) and they cue the search engines to list the site in their results.

While there are special formulas used by the search engines to make their lists and put sites in ranking order, the fact of the matter is that the right choice in keywords can usually make a big difference for any online business.

For instance, if you were to have that psychic site discussed earlier, you would want to investigate the words that turn up the biggest and most profitable sites (your competition) on all search engine results lists. The better PPC sites often help their customers with this issue and can usually guide them to the best choices.

With a good PPC ad in place, you are also going to have to have a "landing page" or "sales letter" that the customer reaches with that single click of their mouse. This means you will have already built a workable and somewhat fluid website around your subject or product. This landing page should allow the visitor to join your membership site, provide an email or purchase a product like an eBook; otherwise you are wasting your effort.

Once you have laid this groundwork, you will begin to be able to track the "click through" rate on your ads. This is usually provided in the form of a percentage rate – for instance, if one thousand people receive the ad after entering their search terms, the click back rate will be the number of those one thousand people who actually clicked. If the ads generate many clicks and a few sales you are probably on the right track, but you will always need to hone and freshen your site.

For example, if you have a high click through rate, but you don't get many sales, you don't need to change the adwords you have selected. You will, however, need to do something about the landing pages or sales letters where the ads lead the customer to, because it is this area that is failing to "close the deal".

Email Communications

Another approach to testing your markets is through direct email communication. Once you have developed a sales letter or landing page with good results, you can then take the basic language and message from that and convert it into an email that you will send to a relevant and targeted email list. There are hundreds of sources for good email lists created for marketing campaigns and, from the start, you should try to find the right agency or site for your needs. Remember too that you will be constantly gathering emails from interested consumers through your sales page, and in the next paragraph we'll address how that is done.

This email can also be a "make or break" tool where traffic and sales will be concerned, so put some real time, thought and effort into making it. Any direct emails must always contain a clickable link or an email address submission option that gives the recipient something in return. This is called "value added" email, and it is one of the smartest ways to create successful marketing campaigns, such as targeted emails. It also allows you to develop and build specific email lists.

For instance, if we still use the psychic-oriented membership website as an example, we could include a free astrology chart or eBook for all people who follow the link and submit an email address. These email addresses would automatically come to the website owner with the code or details about the ad or direct email that brought the consumer to the site. With such information, it becomes quite easy to identify customers into specific groups of interest. Such as tarot-oriented groups or astrology groups, etc.

Understanding the Goals

Ultimately, the goal of your efforts is to create results that are "self-sustaining", which means that the real work in obtaining reliable traffic with high "conversion" rates will eventually occur mostly through the powerful search engine results.

Perhaps it is a bit helpful to give a quick explanation of the previous paragraph and why this part of creating the membership website is so vital and significant. Firstly, conversion rates mean the number of people who visit the website (due to an email or PPC or banner ad) and then who register or make a purchase.

If the subject has broad appeal, there is likely to be a continuing level of interest and visitation – which can make the membership site somewhat self-sustaining. Once regular customers begin to frequent the site, purchase the products and spread the word, it will also allow the website owner to take a few steps back from the hardest part of the marketing work.

In addition to this, however, there are going to be other ways of getting people to know about your membership site, like blogs, articles and links, but these will not be a focus in this work. Why not? Because there are other approaches to membership websites that are much more targeted and reliable, including the use of wholesale memberships, audio programs, and even reprint materials that spread the word about the website and constantly attracts new members.

Remember that this section began as a discussion about testing the markets, and if you apply the principles covered, you will be able to really hone your marketing and advertising efforts. This takes constant evaluation and assessment to accomplish, but if you do some tweaking here and there and measure which letters, emails, landing pages, products and services generate the biggest surge of interest; then you are well on your way to success.

The Top Five

As mentioned earlier in this book, there are a few essential and basic tools that must be used by anyone hoping to develop a successful membership website. These are not going to necessarily be something entirely familiar to people who currently own or operate retail or sales-oriented websites because membership-based sites are not always geared towards the same results.

Remember that you must have a constant flow of valuable information at the membership site if you want members to continue making their regular monthly payments or purchasing new materials.

For example, it is important to note that some of the most famous membership websites include national newspapers and magazines that offer daily updates and alternative media.

The "Top Five Tools" are: regular audio workshops, interviews and "webinars"; development of special resources; regular or frequent offerings of member discounts; reprint and resale rights materials; and selling wholesale memberships. All five topics are going to be thoroughly reviewed in the succeeding sections of this work.

While eventually implementing all of them will cement your success, it is obviously not possible to tackle everything at one time. First, you should review the tools and topics and implement those you feel are most relevant to your audience or market.

For example, our fictional psychic membership website would benefit most from weekly and exclusive interviews or webinars with famous or notable individuals in the field. These could be streamed to registered members via RSS, or they could be downloadable files at the website. Either way, it is something that keeps the customer coming back for more and continuing to making those membership payments.

Regular Audio Programs, Interviews and Webinars

If you are a frequent Internet surfer, you will know that words on the screen are not the only way that information is delivered. There are all kinds of streaming media that are easy to create and which give a membership website some added value. Currently there are web videos and audio recordings of all kinds as well as downloadable books and other materials.

As an Internet entrepreneur you may need to think like a talk show host as well, and find ways to offer your members access to an ever-increasing and deeply interesting library of audio programs and interviews. It also helps to consider interactive forums and "webinars" in which the members can login and participate.

What should all of these materials be about? Well, consider that you are going to view your subject matter in terms of the broadest scope possible. So, if we once again consider our psychic membership website we can offer interviews with psychics, palm readers, experts on the occult and even ghost hunters.

How would you get all of these interviews? Well, this is the real beauty of using such a method for marketing and enhancing your membership website. You will be able to approach any potential interview or expert with a fairly valuable offer, and this is that they are getting all kinds of free publicity through their participation. Subsequently, their expertise gives the website high-quality information, exclusive materials, and a definite measure of authority over other similar sites.

In addition to providing the benefits noted above, your interaction with experts and contributors is going to constantly bring you into contact with materials and products that you can offer to members at exclusive prices through your website. Remember, that these materials and products are items that your interview subjects are going to really want to sell, and so they are getting both the benefit of the free publicity as well as access to a targeted audience and market.

As an example, consider the psychic who agrees to an interview. Their specialty might be the use of tarot cards, phrenology or palm reading, but whatever it is you will be able to offer registered members of the site special access to the discussion. This could be in the form of an audio file, article or even a transcript. The actual interview could be announced through a members-only newsletter and also through a special emailing to all registered addresses.

You might even ask your members to submit questions about any related issue.

Along with the interview, the site would also market the expert's products or materials. For instance, that psychic mentioned above might extend special pricing on tarot reading services, special charts or even eBooks to members of your site. These member bonuses will always need to be real deals and bargains that are unavailable elsewhere on the Internet.

This makes the membership website a good resource for information, and also keeps the members returning to the site on a regular basis.

The most important issue to remember about all of these materials is the ability to actually market and own them outright. In order to obtain this, you will need to get signed permission and ownership of those things you are going to sell. This gives you the copyright as well as the ability to sell reprint rights at a later date – which is another income stream to be discussed a bit later.

By creating and developing this exclusive and members-only library of materials, you are giving the site an authority that will be difficult to match. You will also be making it a real resource for those looking for detailed and valid information about the subject. This is something that will continually bring in new members who might be scouting out factual and trustworthy articles, interviews or products about your particular subject matter.

Resources

If a membership website is going to be of particular use to its registered members, it is going to always aim at providing them with tools and materials they cannot find anywhere else. As just discussed above, this can happen easily through an ever-growing library or encyclopedia of exclusive information and materials. Additionally, this can be achieved by offering free and beneficial items such as computer programs, related links, graphics files and whatever other special items your audience might appreciate.

For example, we'll once again turn to the psychic website. The members of such a site would appreciate links that might take them to such things as a good search engine for haunted locations, a list of psychic oriented events and organizations, and a few fun things like links to magic supply stores or some "how to" articles. They would also appreciate freeware that would be related to their interests as well, for instance there are all kinds of downloads for identifying stars in the night sky, reading palms and even a few fun games. Such things would definitely be of interest to the membership of our fictional site.

The point of the resources is to offer useful and relevant tools that do not fit in with the library of materials, and to make sure that these are always available and working. For instance, if you offer links to other sites you will need to frequently check that the links are working. You should also see if you can "swap" links with the sites you have listed because this actually helps your Internet search engine rankings.

Today's search engines take a huge number of factors into consideration when determining their results, and many links at other sites are actually detected by the search engines. When they are detected, it gives the website what the engines consider "authority". This means that they will have a higher ranking than a site without any shared links.

How do you keep track of all of this extra information? There is a sure-fire approach to doing all of this without too much trouble or effort, and that is to simply catalog every activity you do while building the site. You can make a simple notebook or even a big spreadsheet which itemizes codes, tools, links, articles, site and more.

You must do this because it is going to bring you into direct contact with an endless supply of valuable resources and connections that you can slowly share with your members. For example, if you happen to stumble on a particularly interesting website or article early in the process, you should add this to your organized listing and then eventually add this to the resources area.

If you always keep in mind that membership is never going to be a permanent thing unless the content is current, valid and valuable, you will understand the significance of constantly acquiring and improving your website's resources.

Monthly Discounts for Members Only

We have discussed the importance of offering exclusive and unique materials and also including a handy section full of interesting and valuable resources. While giving free links and members-only access to your collection of exclusive documents, files and materials is a great idea, you are going to find that "back end products" are a fabulous opportunity as well.

What are back end products? Essentially, anything that can be sold or marketed through your membership site which is directly associated with your work can be viewed as a back end product.

Need an example? Let's consider an actual seminar that our psychic website has conducted. They may have booked a venue, scheduled a slate of speakers, and made all of the arrangements to record the entire production. Before the day arrives, they will offer special seminar packages to their members that include eBooks and printed materials, and even some CDs of other documents that will add value to their experience. This is a back end product, but so too will be the

CDs, downloads, eBooks and other items that can be developed following the end of the seminar. All of the recordings can be marketed along with a "workbook" or other items to those who could not attend, and also as one of the company's regular products.

Of course, back end products can also come through collaborative arrangements with your interview subjects and shared link providers. For instance, a guest may offer some steep discounts to your members if they enter a special code during the checkout process.

Alternately, they might extend special pricing on services through your site as well.

The great thing about such arrangements is that you will be able to pursue any sort of connections and arrangements while offering a pre-existing market and free publicity. We did mention this earlier where the interview subjects were concerned, but this same thing will apply to anyone who helps you offer your members regular access to discounted products and services that are innovative or valuable.

In addition to membership bonuses, like the discounted goods and services, there should also be free member bonuses too. Here is where the website owner can use a variety of materials to supplement newsletter information or even promote other products. For example, the first few chapters of one eBook can be edited into a "freebie" which then encourages the reader to purchase the subsequent books, or chapters as well.

It is important to ensure that any member bonus products are valuable and original because it often happens that freebies end up being valueless or of low-quality which soon discourages some members who may then end their subscriptions.

Reprint and Resale Rights

So far, we have looked at original materials that only you and your members will have direct access to. Clearly, such tools are going to demand a considerable amount of thought, planning and work in order to create, but they all are well-worth it in the end. Now, we can look at pre-packaged items that provide unlimited and copyright free access to eBooks, sales letters, CDs, software downloads and more. These are referred to as reprint and resale rights products and are among one of the hottest things in modern marketing.

How do they work? Well, you would have to take some time to scout out the materials most suitable to your audience, and the Internet is chock-full of such resources. Be a bit cautious, however, because there is currently a real over-abundance of material and you really want to commit your time and resources to the most relevant and the most unique.

For example, a membership website owner could easily acquire exclusive rights to resell an eBook of a few hundred pages. While this might sound great, any responsible and dedicate website owner would take the time to actually read the materials, edit them to their preferences and then repackage it in the finest way possible.

This is something easily done because most of the materials sold as reprint and resale rights products are easy to customize and amend. For instance, a clever owner could take that three or four hundred page eBook and divide it into several smaller works that could be packaged with related workbooks or downloadable audio files. This is entirely legal and a common occurrence among the most savvy membership website owners.

Because the files sold through reprint and resale rights websites are usually very affordable they are frequently used as "freebies" or promotional materials as well, but they should always be thoroughly scrutinized for quality, value and authority before sending them to a potential customer.

Remember too that you will want to also consider the reprint and resale rights products as a valid income stream, and you will eventually find yourself marketing all of them through PPC ads or special email offers as well. These materials are not going to fall under the same category as the discounted products offered to members, because they will usually come directly from you – the website owner – and have no affiliation with any other site or professional.

Statistics around the use of these materials are quite revealing, and somewhere in the area of ninety-five percent of the files are never used or even opened by those who purchase them (either to resell or even as a packaged product). Why this is the case has not yet been identified, but what it does indicate is that you should work hard to create materials that are irresistible and will be read by each person who receives them.

In addition to the reprint and resale rights products, some of these same sites also provide what are frequently referred to as "private label" items also. Usually these are article collections from quality writers who have knowledge about their subject matter. These are usually sold only to the individual willing to purchase them in bulk, and who can then assign their own name in the position of the author. These articles can appear in newsletters, eBooks, various other publications, and even be used to improve search engine results.

It is important to ensure that the articles are of good and trustworthy quality, and if they are, they are sure to become a valuable asset. It is impossible to explain the value of expertise and authority in any membership website materials. If you always keep this in mind when selecting, editing and repackaging articles or reprint and resale rights products you will be sure to make all of the right decisions.

Wholesale Memberships

Lastly we come to one of the more interesting ways of obtaining a nice income through your site and also ensuring a consistent audience – wholesale memberships. Rather than focusing on a person by person membership market, some Internet entrepreneurs insist that you are much better off selling wholesale licenses to those who want to earn some income from the success and quality of the membership website.

How does it work? Basically, the membership website will not sell the individual memberships, but instead will have their registered affiliates do this work for them. The arrangements can vary from site to site, but generally the way it will work is that a website owner will offer bulk membership licensing through which an affiliate acquires several hundred memberships at a discounted price. They will then sell and maintain the memberships through their own site.

Is this profitable? That is a somewhat difficult question to answer. While many membership website owners have found that it is difficult to manage the financial transactions around a membership - there is the initial sale, the establishment of the account, and the maintenance that is required in the event a member fails to pay their monthly fee or lets their subscription expire; there are some who don't mind this level of participation. This means that someone is going to have to be willing and able track the data and make any regular, even daily, amendments to the system. This is the reason that some membership website owners decide to sell bulk memberships rather than collect monthly payments and handle all of their accounts.

For example, if our fictional psychic website decided to use wholesale memberships, it would have a link where someone could purchase a membership. This link, however, would navigate to an affiliate site that had purchased the license to sell and manage memberships for the site. Sure, the monthly income is lost to the website owner, but the work and management also disappears too. Remember too that they did not just give away the memberships, they were sold at bulk pricing, and under fairly rigid guidelines as well. Each time the link is clicked, the guest is transferred to the next affiliate in line, which ensures that all affiliates get a fair chance at taking in new customers.

If you decide to utilize this clever system, you will have to ensure that your affiliates follow the protocols you desire. For instance, you can insist that memberships are never given away for free, because that immediately diminishes the power and value of the other purchased memberships, and opens up your library of information and materials to abuse.

Most membership website owners who opt to use this valuable tool will need to also offer some assistance with the setup process. For example, indexing and payment arrangements are going to require some support. For this reason, it is important to note that selling bulk memberships will still ask the website owner for customer support work on a regular basis.

It is a wise idea to carefully craft some sort of agreement around the terms that must be followed by both parties. For instance, the membership website owner can set the value of the membership and ask that all memberships be sold at their minimum value or be offered only as a premium of the same value. They can also guarantee the varieties of customer support available from the membership website – such as help with payment arrangements.

Currently, many companies opt for wire transfers because they are the easiest approach to global business. Payment processing sites can be quite difficult to navigate and obtain coding and software from them is usually a challenge. Currently there are many alternate options through which affiliate marketers and bulk membership sellers are able to accept payments and track their commissions. If you are going to provide wholesale memberships to interested parties, you should make a point of offering links or details about the best payment processors in your country or region.

Something to remember is that all memberships begin and end with the membership website, the affiliates selling them and managing them will have no control over the content of the site and will have to abide by your arrangements or face a termination of their access.

Chapter 3 – Getting Started

Begin at the Beginning

Now that you have a basic outline of the work and tools necessary for the development of a workable membership website, it is time to really dig in and get started. This chapter is going to discuss some choices that you will face and some of the smartest options to follow. We will look at assembling your website; recognizing value; working with words; testimonials; and the day to day details and glitches.

Assembly

Your website is going to begin to feel like a great big puzzle, and you must assemble many of the major pieces before it begins to really look like something. This means that you must be sure you have these necessary pieces before you begin the process of building the site, and this will always include knowledge as well as equipment and resources.

The knowledge you should really try hard to acquire as quickly and efficiently as possible will include marketing basics, and website infrastructure. For instance, you know that you should compose some sales letters, website content and choose adwords, but how do you start this process? You also know you need a gateway through which members will visit the site, make their purchases or establish their recurring payments (if you decide to sell the memberships through the site rather than through an affiliate). This means you will need to understand where these things can be located.

So, let's look at the "physical" site first.

Send Me a Programmer!

Most Internet entrepreneurs quickly realize that they are going to need some guidance and support from a qualified programmer who can help them to setup the many processes that must occur through their site. While there are an enormous number of web hosting companies offering all kinds of ecommerce sites, they may not provide the kind of integrated services demanded of a membership website (i.e. the membership database, login software, library of numerous media types, and more).

What most membership website owners fail to realize is that they should work in a backwards direction – they should work with a programmer to design the system, rather than purchasing various programs and sites and then demanding that the programmer make them all work cohesively.

Additionally, a good programmer will probably have all kinds of connections and resources for additional areas of the website as well. For instance, you will need to record telephone and "live" conversations to be converted into downloadable files. You will need to understand how to work with video recordings, PDF files and more as well. Finding a good and reliable set of professionals to walk you through this setup process is going to save you an enormous amount of time and money.

This means you should sit down and really scrutinize your plans in order to identify all of the equipment, software and gadgets you will need. Then meet with your programmer to work out all of the technical details of the site and establish the best approaches to use for your various media requirements.

Unfortunately, many successful membership website owners admit that they spent large sums of their capital on costly services and equipment that they did not need to purchase or use. They learned through painful experience that there were far less expensive options and even some that were more efficient than those they identified on their own.

This leads to the next phase in the getting started process – recognizing value.

Recognizing Value

As a membership website owner, you will soon realize that you can find a purpose or value to almost every interaction, discussion or tool you see. Recognizing value that will benefit your site is an important skill. It helps to categorize such information however, if it will eventually help you achieve your goals. Earlier in this book we recommended that all membership website owners make a comprehensive list of the steps they made while researching and building their site. This was something that would help to keep the resources available to the members fresh and unique. This is where you should also keep your lists and notes about valuable connections, discussions and ideas too.

For example, even if an interview has gone badly, there are going to be quotes and paragraphs that can be used elsewhere.

Consider that you will probably interview subjects for twenty minutes or more, and if there is little information given or if the subject of the interview was a bit dull, you can still insert some of their statements into newsletters, web content, articles or more. Value is everywhere, but you have to be open minded and creative in order to use it to its fullest degree.

This concept of "recognizing value" also applies to the materials you offer. If you really, sincerely want to succeed, then you are going to have to scrutinize everything posted for members to view. Regardless of your subject matter – psychics, horses, shoes or marketing – your membership website should always be viewed as a true informational resource or a "one stop" destination for learning, interaction and more.

This means you should always keep a watchful eye for those items and materials that will be of value to your site and your members. Once again, let us turn to the fictional psychic website as an example. As the owner, you would want to always keep an open mind about the sort of "stuff" that would interest your membership. This might mean that you would consider posting "how to" articles about photographing ghosts or spirits just as much as you would consider providing your customers with an eBook you found about reading ancient runes.

Working with Words

Until you are really comfortable with the process of writing your ads, emails, website content and eBooks, you should consider hiring a "pro". There are all kinds of online agencies offering very high-quality writing services specifically geared to Internet businesses.

For instance, a website owner could hire a writer or copywriting service to craft "private label" articles, different eBooks, all of their sales letters and landing pages and even their newsletters if necessary. The most important thing to remember about such a choice, however, is that you are receiving the work of a writer, but not necessarily a specialist. If you want to truly create exclusive materials and offerings you will still have to do the research to understand your subject and constantly expand the amount of information you are making available through your site.

How can you be sure to do this? Well, most successful membership website owners actually take the time to sit down and write out the various descriptions, goals and concepts surrounding the creation of their site. Getting very specific on paper is a great way to understand the true subject matter of the site and this, in turn, clarifies such things as keywords for ads and even subjects for articles, books, interviews and more.

Once you understand this, it is much easier to assign specific writing work to professional writers, or begin doing some of this on your own. If you find that a writer or agency is sending a lot of "fluff" to you, you will want to nip this in the bud instantly because your readers will soon discover this as well. Remember, many will have joined because they have a specific level of interest in the subject and are likely to have a pre-existing level of knowledge too.

They will understand quite early on if they are not getting high-quality materials and experiences from their membership.

A good way to ensure you are doing your job well is to visit your competition. In fact, visit the most successful sites with the same subject or general coverage. What sort of items do they offer? Who are they interviewing? What do they discuss in their forums or newsletters? This is a great way to address timely issues and also expand upon the sort of coverage provided by your competitors.

Finally, one of the most crucial and measurable areas of success or failure where words are concerned is in your ad copy. Actually, it is the ad copy that can really determine the success or failure of the membership website altogether. This is due to the fact that even the best written PPC ads cannot seal the deal where a purchase or submission of an email is concerned if the sales letter or landing page is terrible.

How do you write a strong landing page? If you followed the steps discussed a bit earlier in this section – outlining the goals and concepts for the site – you should be able to powerfully summarize these in the ad copy. For example, we can say that our psychic website is directed strongly towards "readings" of various kinds. If the ad copy cannot explain that the site is a one-stop resource for information and training in how to do such readings, then the copy is a total failure.

Basically, the power of any ad copy comes in getting the message across clearly and convincingly. You could be offering a fantastic deal to your members, but if you don't express this well in the ad copy you will not make many sales.

Don't be afraid to direct a chunk of your capital or operating costs towards the preliminary composition of your sales letters, landing pages and ad copy. This is an area that is going to receive a great deal of "tweaking" before you nail it, and if you start with some strong, clear and professional writing you will probably be giving yourself a nice advantage. You might also be saving yourself a lot of marketing money because your writer, or you yourself, may identify some of the ad and keywords you failed to recognize as well.

There is one thing you must NEVER hire a professional writer to do, and that is to compose a testimonial, and we'll discuss why in the next section.

Testimonials

In our modern and somewhat cynical world, do people really believe testimonials? Actually, you only need to look at the success rates of infomercials to understand that people accept even the most gushing and forced testimonials. Why this is so is up for debate, but usually it has to do with the psychological reaction to someone speaking about their experience or opinion. The reason that a testimonial should not be fictional, however, is that it may end up sounding too full of "hype" and sales copy, and this can actually work against the site altogether.

How do you get real and honest testimonials? One of the best ways to acquire valid and honest testimonials is to give away some of your products or materials in exchange for some "feedback". You will have to include a release that allows you to post the user's response or testimonials, and if you receive positive responses then you should post as many as possible.

What if you receive negative feedback? Don't post this anywhere for the public to see, but do use it to address any flaws or weaknesses with your materials or your website. Always thank the contributor (whether the comments were negative or positive), and always ask for permission to reprint their words.

Something that is hugely successful with many membership websites are video and audio testimonials. These can be plugged right into the landing page and automatically launched when opened in any browser. When people hear the actual spoken words of a satisfied customer or website member, it is significantly more powerful than even a well written testimonial. Using audio and video on the site will also give it a level of quality and technology that will usually be impressive.

In addition to posting positive testimonials in the website, use them in such things as sales letters, ads, newsletters and even blogs or articles as well. They are a great way to communicate in "plain speak" to your public and to encourage new memberships and purchases.

Day To Day Details and Glitches

Okay, we have looked at some of the broader ideas of getting started and now we are down to the proverbial "nitty gritty". This includes such things as administrative work, customer support, contact lists, updates and test driving your site on a regular basis.

The administrative work of running a membership website is going to vary from site to site and owner to owner. If you have worked with a programmer and outsource some technical tasks, you are still going to put in a chunk of time each day tackling customer contact emails and support issues. Remember that any of this work will be in addition to all of the interviewing, marketing, writing and other efforts necessary to make your site a really winner.

Early on in this work we recommended working to develop each of the "top five" tools at a rational and orderly pace in order to be sure you had handled them effectively. If you have done this, then you will have created a site that is designed to eventually almost run itself with only minimal input from the owner. As stated, you will need to respond to customers or members to answer questions, but this can be seen as a valuable experience and one that can produce some unique opportunities.

For instance, direct interaction with your public can introduce new topics to cover or identify weaknesses in the site or content, but is a great way to participate in the day to day management. You should really aim at using the questions to develop an FAQ area (frequently asked questions) because this can save you some serious time down the road. Additionally, the questions you field may indicate a pattern of interest and this can really help you to direct customers to areas of the site where the most sales will be possible as well.

In addition to direct contact through customer support, you are going to also need to keep a watchful eye on all of your contact lists. You may be paying for email campaigns and you will always want to be sure that very few are wasted emails heading to former customers or those who do not respond. You are going to also want to make sure that you have identified all possible contacts and emails for your needs, and this is something that could receive some attention every single day. Looking for more relevant contacts may even bring you in touch with interview subjects or partners who can provide you with email lists, but also quality materials or products to be offered to members at discounted prices.

While scheduling an hour for contact development each day is not necessarily a mandatory activity, monitoring and updating the membership website is a definite requirement. Make sure the content is very fresh – with at least one new item for your members to peruse each week.

It is also a great idea to always have a "coming soon" section which alerts them to any seminars, interviews, sales or new products that you will be introducing. Remember, however, that if you are going to revamp your site, this is something that should go out in a widespread email, but not as a "warning"; rather it should be viewed as an exciting expansion or development.

If you do have major plans for the site, and even before you first allow members to begin registering, you should make a point of giving the site and all of its features a real "test run". This means using your own PPC ads, sales letters and landing pages, links, login processes and more in order to ensure that each process is clear, easy and efficient. You will want to do this on a regular basis, particularly if you are changing anything about key processes and functions.

Chapter 4 – Conclusion

This book has aimed at providing you with the real details of developing a successful membership website, and if you have gleaned the basic points, you will understand that the Internet is one of the most powerful ways to create a business. You will be able to use existing technologies and ideas to quickly create a workable website with many enhanced features, and you will be able to find all kinds of resources that can make your site truly unique, valuable and distinctive. The thing to really remember is that you don't have to re- invent the wheel to make a good and successful membership website.

The Internet can really help you with everything you will need because it will allow you to scout out ideas, form partnerships and find information at little cost and in a very short period of time. You have also probably realized that time is a huge factor with online business, and you get even less time to make the deal than with traditional printed marketing

51

materials. For this reason you must try hard to implement and use the various "tools" discussed throughout this book.

If you take the guidelines and recommendations of this work into consideration when you develop your membership website, you will see measurable results almost immediately. Soon, your site will be somewhat self-sustaining due to the consistent audience and growing membership list.

Printed by Libri Plureos GmbH in Hamburg,
Germany

9 785349 818837